WOULD YOU RATHER

SEX EDITION

ARE YOU READY TO PLAY?

some of the questions are from the website:
2023 WOULDURATHERQUESTIONS.COM

RULES!

1. The game can be played in pairs or in larger groups.

2. The first person (A) asks a question to the second person (B).

3. If the first person (A) guesses correctly the answer of the second person (B), they have sex in the given position shown on the next page. If not, the players move on to the second question (you can write the answer on a piece of paper or have it in your head).

4. After one question the players swap and player (B) asks player (A).

WE WISH YOU A GREAT GAME AND EVEN BETTER SEX

Would you rather send your nudes to a stranger

OR

send your nudes to an ex?

YOUR KAMA SUTRA POSITION

6

Would you rather get oral sex

OR

give oral sex?

YOUR KAMA SUTRA POSITION

8

Would you rather be blindfolded

OR

handcuffed during sex?

9

YOUR KAMA SUTRA POSITION

10

Would you rather be terrible at kissing

OR

oral sex?

11

YOUR KAMA SUTRA POSITION

12

Would you rather have sex on a busy bus

OR

in a busy bus's dirty bathroom?

13

YOUR KAMA SUTRA POSITION

14

Would you rather your significant other striptease in public for strangers

OR

striptease in private for friends?

15

YOUR KAMA SUTRA POSITION

16

Would you rather have sex with someone who never showers

OR

someone who never brushes their teeth?

17

YOUR KAMA SUTRA POSITION

18

Would you rather have sex in the shower

OR

sex in the car?

YOUR KAMA SUTRA POSITION

20

Would you rather have a high body count

OR

be with someone that has a high body count?

YOUR KAMA SUTRA POSITION

22

Would you rather sleep with someone of the same sex who's a billionaire and super hot

OR

sleep with someone of the opposite sex who's broke and ugly?

23

YOUR KAMA SUTRA POSITION

24

Would you rather work at a strip club

OR

have a partner who works at a strip club?

25

YOUR KAMA SUTRA POSITION

26

Would you rather have a partner who makes you moan really loudly in bed

OR

a partner who moans really loudly in bed?

27

YOUR KAMA SUTRA POSITION

28

Would you rather talk dirty with your lover's brother/sister

OR

flirt with your lover's best friend?

29

YOUR KAMA SUTRA POSITION

30

Would you rather accidentally scream the wrong name in bed

OR

have your partner accidentally scream the wrong name in bed?

31

YOUR KAMA SUTRA POSITION

32

Would you rather have your toes sucked during sex

OR

have your fingers sucked during sex?

33

YOUR KAMA SUTRA POSITION

34

Would you rather eat someone's ass

OR

have your ass eaten?

35

YOUR KAMA SUTRA POSITION

36

Would you rather sleep with someone really old but skilled

OR

someone your age who sucks in bed?

37

YOUR KAMA SUTRA POSITION

38

Would you rather have your sex video leaked

OR

have a video of you touching yourself leak?

YOUR KAMA SUTRA POSITION

40

Would you rather be
with someone who
likes rough sex

OR

be with someone who
likes gentle sex?

41

YOUR KAMA SUTRA POSITION

42

Would you rather
watch your parents
have sex

OR

have your parents
watch you have sex?

43

YOUR KAMA SUTRA POSITION

44

Would you rather have the lights on

OR

off during foreplay?

YOUR KAMA SUTRA POSITION

46

Would you rather have group sex with strangers

OR

with all your exes?

YOUR KAMA SUTRA POSITION

48

Would you rather bring another person in bed

OR

cheat on me?

YOUR KAMA SUTRA POSITION

50

Would you rather watch something erotic with me

OR

read erotica loud, while touching me?

YOUR KAMA SUTRA POSITION

52

Would you rather
have sex with my best
friend

OR

with your best friend?

53

YOUR KAMA SUTRA POSITION

54

Would you rather have early morning sex

OR

late night sex?

YOUR KAMA SUTRA POSITION

56

Would you rather make out with your boss

OR

watch your partner make out with their boss?

57

YOUR KAMA SUTRA POSITION

58

Would you rather be the submissive partner during sex

OR

the dominant partner?

YOUR KAMA SUTRA POSITION

60

Would you rather find out your partner slept with your parent in the past

OR

your ex now sleeps with your parent?

61

YOUR KAMA SUTRA POSITION

62

Would you rather have a one night stand with a pornstar

OR

with your long-term crush?

63

YOUR KAMA SUTRA POSITION

64

Would you rather grant everyone's sexual wishes

OR

have all your sexual wishes granted?

65

YOUR KAMA SUTRA POSITION

66

Would you rather be
choked while
receiving pleasure

OR

choke and slap
someone while giving
it to them?

67

YOUR KAMA SUTRA POSITION

68

YOUR FREE KAMA SUTRA POSITION!

ENJOY!

69

DID YOU LIKE THE GAME? WE'D LOVE IT IF YOU'D BE WILLING TO RATE OUR WORK !

STAY TUNED AND WAIT FOR NEW BOOKS!

CHECK OUT

ALSO JOIN TO OUR INSTAGRAM!

LDaddyArt

Made in the USA
Las Vegas, NV
28 September 2024